Playmakers

Quarterbacks

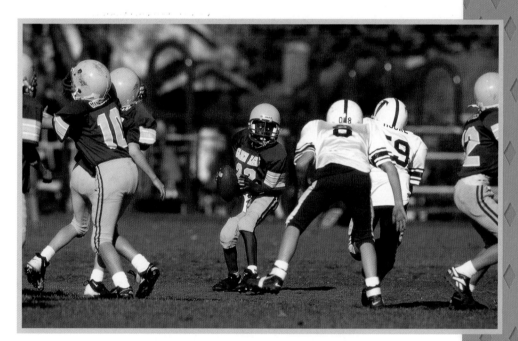

Lynn M. Stone

Rourke
Publishing LLC
Vero Beach, Florida 32964

www.rourkepublishing.com

PHOTO CREDITS: All photos © Lynn M. Stone

Editor: Robert Stengard-Olliges

Cover and page design by Tara Raymo

Library of Congress Cataloging-in-Publication Data

Stone, Lynn M.
 Quarterbacks / Lynn Stone.
    p. cm.
 Includes bibliographical references.
 ISBN 978-1-60044-596-5
 1. Quarterbacking (Football)--Juvenile literature. 2. Quarterbacks (Football)--Juvenile literature. I. Title.
 GV951.3.S76 2008
 796.332'25--dc22

                                    2007019106

Printed in the USA

CG/CG

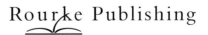

Rourke Publishing

www.rourkepublishing.com – rourke@rourkepublishing.com
Post Office Box 3328, Vero Beach, FL 32964

Table of Contents

The Quarterback

The quarterback on a football team is usually the most important position on a team's **offense**. It is the quarterback who first receives the football from the **center** on almost every play from the line of scrimmage. After receiving the ball from the center, the quarterback has many options.

Positioned at the line of scrimmage, the center snaps the ball to the quarterback.

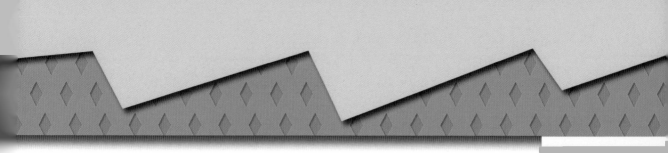

A quarterback must be able to do many things well with a football.

More often than not, the younger age quarterbacks, give the football to a running back. As quarterbacks join high school and college teams, they throw the football more often. Many quarterbacks, including some in high school programs, throw the ball more than they give it to running backs. Certain college and National Football League teams throw the ball about 55 percent of the time.

A quarterback pivots and plants the football in the arms of his running back.

A "pocket" quarterback throws from just steps behind his center.

Quarterbacks usually throw a football from one of three locations. A quarterback may line up directly behind the center for the **snap** of the ball, then retreat a few steps into a pocket. The "pocket" is an area directly behind the center where a quarterback is protected by his blockers. Quarterbacks who regularly throw from a pocket, like most professionals, are "pocket quarterbacks."

A quarterback receives the center's long snap several feet behind the line of scrimmage in a shotgun formation.

A quarterback may also work from a shotgun offense. He stands several steps behind the center to receive the snap. The quarterback then receives the snap in mid-air. In the shotgun offense, the quarterback almost always passes the ball. The advantage of the shotgun is that it immediately places the quarterback further from opposing players.

A roll-out quarterback takes a snap, then dashes either to his right or left, trying to avoid tacklers. He may hold the ball and run with it, or he may throw the ball from behind the line of scrimmage. If a quarterback throws the football forward after he has crossed the line of scrimmage, the pass is illegal and a penalty will follow.

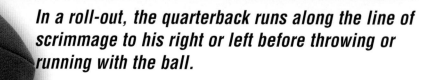

In a roll-out, the quarterback runs along the line of scrimmage to his right or left before throwing or running with the ball.

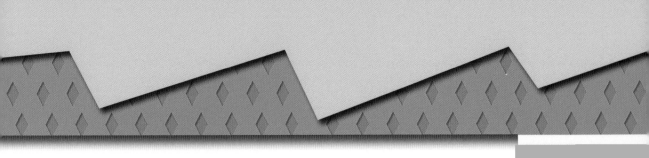

A quarterback must stay behind the line of scrimmage to make a forward pass.

The Quarterback's Skills

Giving the ball to a running back requires perfect timing. The running back usually takes the ball from the quarterback as a **handoff** or **pitch-out**.

A quarterback may pitch the ball to a running back.

On an option play, the quarterback elects whether to run, pass, or pitch out.

A quarterback may also run with the ball himself. Or he may operate an **option** type offense which requires him to first run with the ball, but then consider the option of passing or pitching it to a running back at the last moment.

A quarterback is almost always the player who is responsible for passing the football. Highly skilled passing quarterbacks may pass the ball and complete more than 50 percent of their throws. Throwing a football successfully depends upon the **receiver** catching the throw. It also depends upon the quarterback's talent to throw with speed and accuracy. One measure of speed is release time—the time it takes for a quarterback to take a snap, step up, and throw the football. A high school quarterback should be able to set up and throw a pass within 2.1 to 2.7 seconds. A quarterback gets rid of the ball quickly to avoid being tackled.

Top gun quarterbacks throw often and accurately.

Sure-handed receivers help top quarterbacks complete more than 50 percent of their passes.

Another measure of talent is the speed at which a quarterback can throw a football. Hard throws reach receivers more quickly, but quarterbacks should also be able to throw the ball lightly, too. Especially if the receiver is at close range.

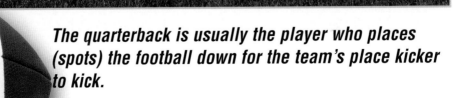

The quarterback is usually the player who places (spots) the football down for the team's place kicker to kick.

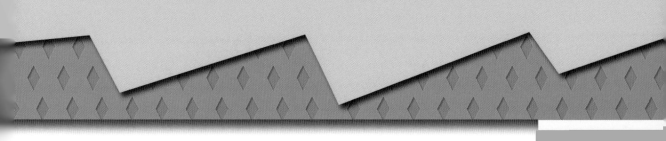

A quarterback needs to have a quick release or he faces the possibility of being tackled, or sacked, by defenders.

Accuracy is important for a quarterback. A quarterback who does not throw accurately is in danger of having a pass **intercepted** by the opposing team.

So, You Want to Be a Quarterback?

Quarterbacks are outstanding athletes. They often play multiple sports. They must be strong, fearless, and capable of throwing a football quickly and accurately. The best quarterbacks are also fast on their feet.

A quarterback's ability to fake a handoff while actually keeping the football can fool the opposing team's defense.

Taller quarterbacks have the advantage of more easily seeing over blockers and opposing rushers.

Quarterbacks are not always big boys or men, but height and muscle are advantages. A quarterback who is tall enough to easily see over his blockers tends to throw with much more accuracy than one who can't. And because they handle the ball, quarterbacks may take a physical beating from frequent tackles.

Listening to the coach, and learning from his experience helps any football player improve.

Beyond the athletic skills required to be a quarterback, a quarterback must be a natural leader. Most quarterbacks don't call the plays; the coach or offensive coordinator calls the play. But a quarterback must **execute** the play, and his teammates must have confidence in his ability.

A quarterback must be able to **"read"** the defense. Looking at the defense and knowing whether to keep the called play or make a change requires experience and practice.

As the field leader, the quarterback must read defenses and sometimes call a new play—an audible—at the line of scrimmage.

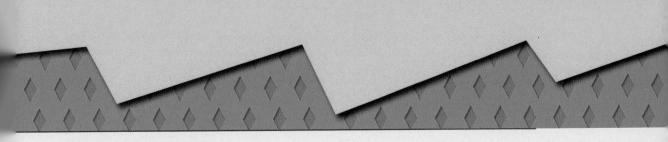

Glossary

center (SEN tur) – the football player along the line who forwards the football to the quarterback

execute (EK suh koot) – to properly carry out a called play

handoff (HAND of) – a ball usually handed from the quarterback to a running back

intercepted (in tur sep TED) – a passed football that was been caught by someone on the opposing team

offense (AW fenss) – the football team with possession of the ball

option (OP shuhn) – refers to a type of offensive formation that allows the quarterback to run, pitch, or throw the football

pitch-out (PICH out) – an underhanded toss of the ball from one back, usually the quarterback, to another running back.

read (REED) – the ability to look at an opposing football formation and recognize its strengths and weaknesses

receiver (ri SEE vur) – the player on the offense who catches a passed football

snap (SNAP) – the motion by which a center either places or throws the football underhanded into a teammate's hands

Index

Further Reading

Grabowski, John F. *Legendary Football Quarterbacks*. Thomson Gale, 2003.
Jenkins, Ron. *Quarterback Play*. Coaches Choice, 2003.
Preller, James. *NFL Super Bowl Super Quarterbacks*. Scholastic, 2005.

Website to Visit

http://www.everything2.com/index.pl?node=quarterback
www.nfl.com/players/playerindex/POS_QB

About the Author

Lynn M. Stone is the author of more than 400 children's books. He is a talented natural history photographer as well. Lynn, a former teacher, travels worldwide to photograph wildlife in its natural habitat.